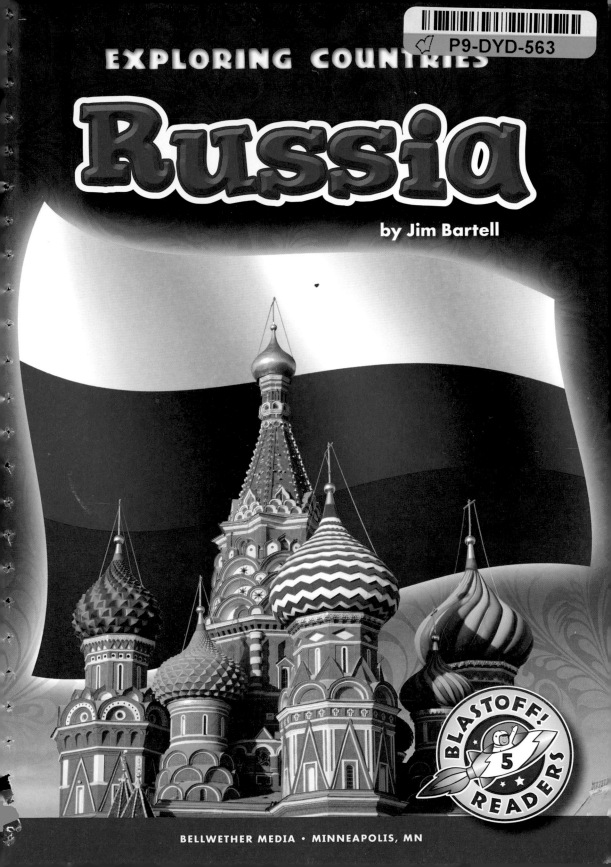

EXPLORING COUNTRIES

Russia

by Jim Bartell

BLASTOFF! READERS
5

BELLWETHER MEDIA · MINNEAPOLIS, MN

Note to Librarians, Teachers, and Parents:

Blastoff! Readers are carefully developed by literacy experts and combine standards-based content with developmentally appropriate text.

Level 1 provides the most support through repetition of high-frequency words, light text, predictable sentence patterns, and strong visual support.

Level 2 offers early readers a bit more challenge through varied simple sentences, increased text load, and less repetition of high-frequency words.

Level 3 advances early-fluent readers toward fluency through increased text and concept load, less reliance on visuals, longer sentences, and more literary language.

Level 4 builds reading stamina by providing more text per page, increased use of punctuation, greater variation in sentence patterns, and increasingly challenging vocabulary.

Level 5 encourages children to move from "learning to read" to "reading to learn" by providing even more text, varied writing styles, and less familiar topics.

Whichever book is right for your reader, Blastoff! Readers are the perfect books to build confidence and encourage a love of reading that will last a lifetime!

This edition first published in 2011 by Bellwether Media, Inc.

No part of this publication may be reproduced in whole or in part without written permission of the publisher. For information regarding permission, write to Bellwether Media, Inc., Attention: Permissions Department, 5357 Penn Avenue South, Minneapolis, MN 55419.

Library of Congress Cataloging-in-Publication Data

Bartell, Jim.
  Russia / by Jim Bartell.
    p. cm. – (Blastoff! readers: Exploring countries)
  Includes bibliographical references and index.
  Summary: "Developed by literacy experts for students in grades three through seven, this book introduces young readers to the geography and culture of Russia"–Provided by publisher.
  ISBN 978-1-60014-488-2 (hardcover : alk. paper)
  1. Russia (Federation)–Juvenile literature. I. Title.
  DK510.23.B37 2010
  947–dc22   2010009212

Printed in the United States of America, North Mankato, MN.

080110   1162

Contents

Arctic Ocean

Norway

Russia

★ Moscow

Black
Sea

Caspian
Sea

Russia is the largest country in the world. It stretches across both Europe and Asia, covering 6,601,668 square miles (17,098,242 square kilometers). The Ural Mountains separate the European and Asian parts of Russia. Fourteen countries border Russia, from Norway in northern Europe to China in southeastern Asia. Russia's capital is Moscow.

Did you know?

At the Bering Strait, the distance between Russia and Alaska is only 53 miles (85 kilometers). The deepest part of the strait is only 165 feet (50 meters) deep.

Alaska

Bering Strait

Pacific Ocean

China

Russia also touches many bodies of water. The Arctic Ocean lies off Russia's northern coast, and the Pacific Ocean lies to the east. The Black Sea and the Caspian Sea, both bordering southwestern Russia, provide access to Europe and the Middle East.

Did you know?

Some Russians live in Siberia, even though it is one of the coldest places on Earth. In the winter, the average temperature ranges from -10 to -50 degrees Fahrenheit (-23 to -45 degrees Celsius).

Russia has large plains, tall mountains, and thick forests. The Eurasian **Steppe** spans much of southwestern Russia. It is a large area of grassland that is too dry to support trees. South of the Eurasian Steppe, the Caucasus Mountains run between the Black and Caspian Seas. Siberia is a region that lies east of the Ural Mountains. Most of Siberia is either **taiga** or **tundra**. Tall evergreen forests cover the ground in the taiga. The ground on the tundra is **permafrost**, which makes farming difficult.

Russia has many rivers. The most important rivers are the Volga, the Yenisey, and the Ob. The Volga is Europe's longest river. Eleven of Russia's largest cities stand on the banks of the Volga.

Lake Baikal is the oldest and deepest freshwater lake in the world. Located in Siberia, it is at least 30 million years old and has a maximum depth of 5,315 feet (1,620 meters). Around 330 rivers flow into the lake, but only one river, the Angara, flows out of it. The Buryat people are native to the land around the lake. They have lived there for hundreds of years.

Scientists are very interested in Lake Baikal. Its age and isolation have protected many rare kinds of plants and animals. More than 1,700 kinds of plants and animals live in Lake Baikal. Most of them cannot be found anywhere else in the world.

Baikal seal

polar bears

Russia has a wide variety of wildlife. Polar bears roam the northern regions of Russia. Brown bears can be seen in the country's warmer areas. There are so many bears in Russia that the bear is often used as a national symbol. Bears are not the only large predators in Russia. Tigers, leopards, and wolves also hunt across Russia's terrain. Minks, ibexes, deer, and **pikas** are often prey for these predators.

Amur leopard

Did you know?
The Amur leopard is one of the rarest wildcats on the planet. Scientists think that only about 30 of these leopards exist in the wild. Amur leopards live in eastern Russia.

pika

Siberian tiger

fun fact
Siberian tigers can grow up to 13 feet (4 meters) long. They can weigh up to 700 pounds (317 kilograms)!

Many animals inhabit the waters in and around Russia. Salmon, sea otters, and beavers swim in Russia's rivers. Sharks, whales, and dolphins can be found off Russia's coasts.

Russia is home to around 140 million people. It is the ninth most populated country in the world. Most of Russia's people are **native** Russians. Their **ancestors**, the Slavic people, lived on the land Russia occupies today.

Speak Russian!

The Russian language uses a different alphabet than English. However, Russian words can be written in the English alphabet so you can read them out loud.

English	Russian	How to say it
hello	zdravstvuyte	zdrast-VOO-yuh-tuh
good-bye	do svidanya	da-svee-DAH-neeyah
yes	da	DAH
no	nyet	nee-YET
please	pozhalusta	pah-ZHA-loo-stuh
thank you	spasiba	spa-SEE-bah
friend (male)	drug	droog
friend (female)	podruga	pah-droo-ga

Other groups of people that live in Russia include Ukrainians and Tatars. Ukrainians have roots in Ukraine, a country that borders western Russia. The Tatars are a group native to parts of central Asia. Both the Ukrainians and the Tatars speak their own languages, but many also know Russian, the official language of Russia. Many people in Russia also speak English.

Most Russians live in apartments in large cities such as Moscow and Saint Petersburg. In these apartments, people often share kitchens and bathrooms with their neighbors. Families are small, usually with only one or two children. If both parents work, young children are often left in the care of a grandmother, or *babushka*. People use cars, motorcycles, and trains to get around the city. They shop at stores, malls, and markets.

Where People Live in Russia

countryside 27%

cities 73%

Many Russians who live in the country are farmers. They live in houses on their farms and shop in small villages. It is becoming more common for young Russians to leave the countryside for jobs in cities. Because of this, Russia's small villages are disappearing.

Did you know?
Some Russians who live in cities have a cabin, or *dacha*, in the countryside where they go to relax.

Because both parents in Russian families usually work, many children between the ages of 3 and 6 are enrolled in preschools. Children are required to go to elementary school, which lasts for nine grades. They learn reading, math, social studies, and other subjects.

After elementary school, students can choose to attend either a school that teaches them job skills or a high school. Students who go to a high school learn science, foreign languages, and advanced math. After graduating, they can apply to universities.

fun fact

Russian children stopped wearing school uniforms in the 1990s. Today, many Russian children wear fur coats to stay warm in cold classrooms.

Where People Work in Russia

manufacturing 31.9%

farming 10%

services 58.1%

Russians who live in cities most often have **service jobs** in offices, stores, and hospitals. Factories also employ many Russians in cities. Factory workers make machinery, chemicals, and **textiles**. These products are used in Russia or sold around the world.

In the countryside, most people are farmers. They grow wheat, corn, sugar beets, and sunflowers. Livestock farmers raise cattle, sheep, and pigs. The countryside also has many **natural resources**. Miners dig into the earth for diamonds, gold, and iron ore. Loggers cut down trees to make lumber. Many Russians work in oil fields throughout the country. Fishermen use big nets to catch fish along Russia's coasts.

fun fact

Russia has produced many chess players who have earned the title of "grandmaster." There are only about 1,100 grandmasters in the world.

During their free time, Russians like to play sports and games, watch TV, and visit friends. Most Russians know how to play chess. Many people enjoy playing with just their friends and family, but the best players enter tournaments held throughout the country.

Soccer, hockey, volleyball, and ice-skating are popular sports in Russia. They all have professional leagues or organizations. Many children begin playing these sports at an early age. The best ice-skaters often grow up to compete in the **Winter Olympics**. Dancing is also a large part of Russian culture. Russian ballet is famous around the world.

Did you know?
Tea is the most popular drink in Russia. Most Russians drink it throughout the day, and it is often served after meals.

Russians enjoy a variety of hearty meals. Soups and stews are especially popular in colder regions of the country. *Borscht* is a soup made with beets and served with sour cream, dill, and green onions. It can be eaten hot or cold. Cabbage soup, or *shchi*, includes other vegetables and is often topped with sour cream. Warm dumplings called *pelmeni* are also a common meal throughout Russia.

Blini are thin pancakes that can be stuffed with jam, honey, cheese, meat, or **caviar**. Pastries called *pirozhki* are another favorite stuffed food. Most are filled with meat and potatoes and then baked in an oven.

caviar

borscht

fun fact

The seventh week before Easter, many Russians do not eat meat. Instead, they eat pancakes! This holiday is called *Maslenitsa*, or Pancake Week. It is also a celebration of the beginning of spring, and the pancakes, or *blini*, are said to symbolize the sun.

Russia celebrates many holidays throughout the year. The national holiday falls on June 12 and is called Russia Day. It is a day to celebrate the end of the **Soviet Union** and the formation of modern Russia.

Victory Day is another important holiday. On May 9, Russians celebrate their victory over the Germans in World War II. Parades are held in major cities, and the country remembers the soldiers who fought to defend Russia. The biggest holiday in Russia is the celebration of the New Year. Russians drink champagne and set off fireworks. They reflect on the past year and look forward to the new one.

Did you know?

Most Christians in Russia are Orthodox Christians. They celebrate Christmas on January 7 because they follow a different calendar than other Christians.

Moscow's Red Square

Saint Basil's Cathedral

Red Square is the center of Moscow and is considered the heart of Russia. All of Moscow's main roads start in Red Square. Famous Russian landmarks surround the square. The Kremlin, a former palace of the kings and queens of Russia, is now the home of the Russian president. Saint Basil's **Cathedral** sits next to the Kremlin. The cathedral's bright colors and onion-shaped domes have made it a national symbol of Russia.

People who live in Moscow often meet to talk in Red Square. Throughout Russia's history, many national celebrations have taken place there. Today, Red Square brings Russians together to remember how the country has overcome challenges and to look forward to a bright future.

Fast Facts About Russia

Russia's Flag

The flag has three horizontal stripes. There is a white stripe on top, a blue stripe in the middle, and a red stripe on the bottom. Peter the Great, a Russian ruler, first used the flag over 300 years ago. In 1917, Russia adopted the flag of the Soviet Union and stopped using this design. After the Soviet Union broke up, Russia went back to the old design on August 21, 1991.

Official Name: Russian Federation

Area: 6,601,668 square miles (17,098,242 square kilometers); Russia is the largest country in the world.

Capital City:	Moscow
Important Cities:	Saint Petersburg, Novosibirsk, Vladivostok, Novgorod
Population:	139,390,205 (July 2010)
Official Language:	Russian
National Holiday:	Russia Day (June 12)
Religions:	None (63%), Christian (22%), Muslim (15%)
Major Industries:	farming, fishing, forestry, manufacturing, mining, services
Natural Resources:	oil, coal, natural gas, wood, iron ore, diamonds, gold
Manufactured Products:	wood products, metals, chemicals, machinery, military technology, clothing
Farm Products:	wheat, corn, sunflowers, potatoes, sugar beets, cattle, sheep, pigs
Unit of Money:	ruble; the ruble is divided into 100 kopeks.

Glossary

ancestors—relatives who lived long ago

cathedral—a large church

caviar—fish eggs; Russian caviar is famous around the world.

native—originally from a place

natural resources—materials in the earth that are taken out and used to make products or fuel

permafrost—ground that is frozen year-round

pikas—small animals similar to rabbits

service jobs—jobs that perform tasks for people or businesses

Soviet Union—a large country in eastern Europe and western Asia that broke up in 1991; Russia was part of the Soviet Union.

steppe—a vast, flat, treeless plain

taiga—land south of a tundra that is covered in evergreen forests

textiles—fabrics or clothes that have been woven or knitted

tundra—frozen, treeless land; beneath the surface, tundra is permafrost, or land that is permanently frozen.

Winter Olympics—a worldwide sporting competition held every four years during the winter

To Learn More

AT THE LIBRARY

De Capua, Sarah. *Russia*. New York, N.Y.: Benchmark Books, 2004.

Fontes, Justine, and Ron. *Russia*. New York, N.Y.: Children's Press, 2003.

Schemenauer, Elma. *Welcome to Russia*. Mankato, Minn.: Child's World, 2008.

ON THE WEB

Learning more about Russia is as easy as 1, 2, 3.

1. Go to www.factsurfer.com.

2. Enter "Russia" into the search box.

3. Click the "Surf" button and you will see a list of related Web sites.

With factsurfer.com, finding more information is just a click away.

Index

The images in this book are reproduced through the courtesy of: Denis Babenko, front cover; Maisei Raman, front cover (flag), p. 28; Ivan Epparski, pp. 4-5; Juan Martinez, pp. 6-7, 8-9, 11 (top), 14, 15, 19 (right), 22, 23 (top), 24, 29 (bill); Konrad Wothe/Photolibrary, p. 9 (small); Marketa Jirouskova/ Photolibrary, pp. 10-11; Adrian Baras, p. 11 (middle); Eduard Titov, p. 11 (bottom); Bruno Morandi/ Getty Images, p. 13; Doctor Kan, p. 16; Shalom Ormsby/Getty Images, p. 17; Tatiana Morozova, p. 18; Frank Siteman/Getty Images, p. 19 (left); Frans Lemmens/Alamy, p. 20; Jonathan Larsen, p. 21; Elzbieta Sekowska, p. 23 (bottom); Peshkov Daniil, p. 25; Gonzalo Azumendi/Photolibrary, p. 26; Helen and Vlad Filatov, p. 27; Sergey Vasilyev, p. 29 (coin).